FAMOUS

D0847845

Prince William

by Sheila Wyborny

KIDHAVEN
PRESS™

THOMSON
———✦———™
GALE

San Diego • Detroit • New York • San Francisco • Cleveland
New Haven, Conn. • Waterville, Maine • London • Munich

© 2003 by KidHaven Press. KidHaven Press is an imprint of The Gale Group, Inc., a division of Thomson Learning, Inc.

KidHaven™ and Thomson Learning™ are trademarks used herein under license.

For more information, contact
KidHaven Press
27500 Drake Rd.
Farmington Hills, MI 48331-3535
Or you can visit our Internet site at http://www.gale.com

LIBRARY OF CONGRESS CATALOGING-IN-PUBLICATION DATA

Wyborny, Sheila, 1950–
    Prince William / by Sheila Wyborny.
        p. cm. — (Famous people)
    Summary: Profiles Prince William of England, whose life blends privilege, official duties, and traditions with a modern upbringing in private schools, youthful horseplay, and private tragedy.
    Includes bibliographical references and index.
    ISBN 0-7377-1401-8 (alk. paper)
    1. William, Prince, grandson of Elizabeth II, queen of Great Britain, 1982—Juvenile literature. 2. Princes—Great Britain—Biography—Juvenile literature. [1. William, Prince, grandson of Elizabeth II, queen of Great Britain, 1982– 2. Princes.] I. Title. II. Series.
        DA591.A45 W568 2003
        941.085'092—dc21
                                                    2002005693

Printed in the United States of America

368-5335

CONTENTS

Chapter One

Always in the Spotlight

He is blond and over six feet tall with movie star looks. Everywhere he goes girls scream and clamor for a glance, a smile, or, in their wildest dreams, a handshake. Bodyguards keep careful watch over his safety. He is not a rock star or a professional athlete. He is His Royal Highness Prince William, the future king of Great Britain, and he has been in the spotlight since the day he was born.

Born Famous

William Arthur Philip Louis Windsor, better known as Prince William, was born on June 21, 1982, in St. Mary's Hospital in London, England. His mother was Princess Diana, formerly Lady Diana Spencer, and his father is Prince Charles, heir to the British throne. William was their first child.

Prince William poses for a photo at Eton, his boarding school.

William's birth was formally announced by a brightly costumed crier, ringing a bell outside the gates of Buckingham Palace. Parties commenced in cities and villages all over Great Britain, and bonfires were lit across the countryside. Not only in Great Britain, but anywhere British subjects lived in the world, the prince's birth was cause for celebration, because this tiny baby would one day be their king.

Like new parents often do, William's parents marveled at the child they had created. Prince Charles wrote to a friend: "He really does look surprisingly appetizing and he has sausage fingers just like mine."[1]

The Royal Baby

Although his parents tried to give him a normal childhood, little about William's life would be normal. On August 4, when William was forty-five days old, members of Britain's two best-known families gathered for William's first official event, his christening. Attending the event were four generations of the Windsor family, including Queen Elizabeth, William's grandmother; the queen mother, William's great grandmother; and Prince Charles's brothers and sister. Also present were Princess Diana's relatives, including her mother, Frances Shand Kydd, who was divorced from Diana's father, Edward Spencer (also known as the Earl Spencer). Everyone assembled in the music room of Buckingham Palace for William's christening.

For the ceremony, William wore a gown that had been worn for the christening of every future British

Young Prince William steadies himself on his father's knee as Princess Diana looks on.

king since Edward VII in 1841. The silver-trimmed baptismal font, usually exhibited in the Tower of London, was brought to Buckingham Palace for the event.

Although William behaved well for the christening, he was tired, hungry, and out of patience by the time the ceremony ended. During a photography session afterward, he cried and cried. His grandmother, Queen Elizabeth, remarked that he was a good speech maker. His great grandmother commented that he had a good pair of lungs. The press dubbed the baby "Prince of Wails," a play on his father's title, Prince of Wales.

Though newborn and totally helpless, the heir to the throne had made his presence known and was already breaking many long-standing traditions.

Breaking Traditions

William's parents had decided early on that his life would be different from that of previous royal babies. They wanted him to grow up in a warm family setting, something neither of them had experienced.

Before William's birth, all royal babies had been born at the palace and reared in a nursery filled with dark, heavy, antique furniture. Charles and Diana decided their baby's birth would take place in a hospital. And when he came home, it would be to a nursery with pastel walls, colorful stuffed animals, and Disney characters.

Nor would William know his nanny better than his own parents. Both Charles and Diana had spent most of their childhoods in the company of nannies. In fact, Charles was with his mother only about an hour a day from the time he was an infant until he was five years old. Charles and Diana both made it clear they would be actively involved in the raising of their children. For William's nanny they chose Barbara Barnes, who had no formal training as a nanny but had experience taking care of children. Barbara understood that Charles and Diana would be fully involved parents and would have a hand in dressing, feeding, and baths whenever possible.

Unlike his father, William would also travel with his parents on some of their trips abroad. As a child, Charles had always stayed with nannies when his parents, Queen Elizabeth and Prince Philip, visited other countries.

William's first big trip with his parents came at age nine months. They traveled on an official visit to Australia and New Zealand. He was the first royal baby to take a royal business trip.

William's first steps are captured on film with the proud parents watching in the background.

Because he was so outgoing, active, and cheerful, William was a big hit with the Australian press and public. Not only had Charles and Diana kept their little family together, they had also won the approval of British subjects at home and abroad.

But life in the public eye was not all fun. Anyone, but particularly a small child, would lose patience with always being in the spotlight. Prince William reacted like any other child might. He was not always Prince "Charming."

Television reporters surround two-year-old Prince William.

Strong-Willed Wills

Prince William, nicknamed Wills by his mother, had his first official visit with the British press at eighteen months. When asked to walk toward the television cameras and reporters, William bolted in the other direction. Not only did he not want to walk for the cameras, he did not want to smile for them, either.

By this time, William's reputation as an active toddler had spread far and wide. He was not more mischievous than most other children his age, but everything he did was broadcast on television or printed in the newspapers. More than once, he scampered away from his nanny and set off alarms at Kensington Palace in London and at the queen's country home at Balmoral Castle in Scotland.

Another incident that was widely reported happened at Birkenhall, his great grandmother's residence in Scotland, when William was about three years old. He stormed into the dining room, tipped over chairs, broke plates, and damaged a portrait of Queen Victoria. William was having a royal toddler tantrum.

Some of William's more amusing antics included crawling into wastebaskets to see what was in them and examining his father's shoes. Prince Charles did not laugh, however, when his small son tried to flush his shoes down the toilet.

But William was not all curiosity and mischief. He could also be thoughtful and helpful. When William was two, his brother Harry was born. From the beginning, William was a loving and protective

Princes William and Harry stroll to Wetherby School.

big brother. His father reported that the two "got along beautifully, right from the first moment."[2]

In many ways William was an average toddler. He had his good moments and his not-so-good moments. But his parents wanted him to develop the kind of manners he would need in dealing with the public and with the press. They also wanted him to have normal relationships with other children. So, when he was three years old, William became the first royal heir to be sent outside the palace to nursery school.

CHAPTER TWO

Educating a Future King

Like most parents, Charles and Diana wanted William to have a good education. And in William's case, he also needed an education that would prepare him for his future as England's king. But Charles and Diana also felt it was important for their son to have the same types of childhood experiences that other children have.

Said a family friend, "Charles and Diana want William, and later Harry, to have as normal an existence as possible."[3]

Learning to Get Along

On September 24, 1985, at three years, three months of age, William became the first royal heir to attend nursery school away from the palace. His parents chose Mrs. Mynor's Nursery School, only ten minutes from their home at Kensington Palace. At school he would simply be called William, not Prince William, and would sit at a table with six other children. His first school project, which he proudly brought home to his mother, was a paper mouse.

William did make friends, as his parents hoped he would. His best friend, and partner in mischief, was named Nicholas. Instead of painting on their paper, sometimes William and Nicholas painted each other's faces. And once they tried to flush a classmate's lunch down the toilet.

Aside from occasional mischief, William's overall behavior improved and so did his manners.

When he "graduated" from nursery school, his parents enrolled him at a nearby private elementary school called Wetherby. In January 1987 William ar-

Britain's two princes play on a fire engine.

Walking alongside his parents, Prince William makes his way to a wedding.

rived at Wetherby to the glare of newspaper and television cameras. He was four-and-a-half years old.

In class with twenty other boys William learned math, geography, French, reading, and computers, but his favorite subject was art. He liked to draw castles and military scenes.

William attended Wetherby for four years. While there, he developed thoughtfulness toward others. The parent of a classmate said, "I've often seen Prince William comforting a young child who's clearly unhappy. He'll talk earnestly to him and make sure he's all right before resuming playing. He really does think of others."[4]

Away from school, William enjoyed swimming. He won a swimming award when he was seven years old. He also enjoyed riding his pony, Trigger. Trigger was kept at Highgrove, the family's country home. William entered his first riding competition in 1988 and was named third best rider.

William's grandmother, the queen, was pleased that William had taken to horseback riding because she enjoyed it as well. When time permitted, the two liked to ride together.

Away from Home

By the time he was eight, William was ready to begin more serious academic study as well as training for his future. On September 10, 1990, William entered Ludgrove, an exclusive prep school in Berkshire, twenty-five miles from London. Ludgrove, an all-boys school, was also a boarding school. William would live at the school weekdays and go home every Friday.

Although it was difficult to leave his home and family, William soon settled into his daily routine. Everyone rose at 7:15 A.M., went to classes, ate in the dining hall together, played sports, and went to sleep at 8 P.M.

For the most part, William was treated the same as the other 186 boys. He followed the same rules and, like the other boys, received ten dollars a month allowance. The one obvious difference between William and his classmates was the presence of a bodyguard. No matter where William went, a bodyguard followed. This was a standard precaution for all members of the royal family.

The Public and Private Prince

William was popular with both teachers and classmates. He participated in sports, representing his school in

William and Harry wave to the press.

cross-country running, and was captain of his school's hockey and rugby teams. He also played soccer.

But sometimes William still had to be a prince and make public appearances at special ceremonies. He performed his first official duty while still a student at Ludgrove. On March 1, 1991, William took a day off

While on vacation over the Easter holiday, the young princes ski at Lech, Austria.

from school to travel to Wales. He unveiled a large plaque in the city of Cardiff. The plaque was to promote commerce and culture in the city. He performed like a true prince, smiling and shaking hundreds of hands. But he was glad when the formalities ended and he could get back to school and his friends.

When not attending classes or studying, William liked to ride his BMX bicycle, skateboard, ride horses, and play tennis. He also like to play "ditch the bodyguard," causing the royal security staff some anxious moments. This problem was solved by means of an electronic homing device he was made to wear at all times.

Parents Apart

While his years at Ludgrove were mostly positive, it was during this time that his parents separated. Though it was not well known outside the immediate family, they had been having problems with their marriage for several years. Diana went to Ludgrove to tell William that she and his father were separating, so he would hear it from her before it became public. She would use Kensington Palace in London as her main residence, and his father would live at Highgrove. William knew that his parents had been unhappy together, and their arguments had caused a lot of tension for the whole family. He told his mother he really thought she and his father would be happier apart. William was already showing some of the wisdom he would need as England's future king.

The prince and princess gaze in opposite directions at a formal event. Diana visited William at Ludgrove to tell him of the royal separation.

Both publicly and privately, William's life had undergone many changes in just a few short years. There were more changes to come.

Eton

William entered Eton College in September 1995. Eton is an exclusive boarding school for wealthy English youth. Although it is called "college," it is for students at the middle school and high school grade levels. Students who wish to attend must pass a difficult twelve-part exam. William scored in the top half of the applicants.

William was a bright student. He made good grades in most of his subjects and was popular with the other students.

By this time, William was attracting the attention of many young girls too. Besides being a royal prince and future king, he had a bright smile, blue eyes, and a shy, sideways glance like his mother. His brother and his classmates sometimes called him Dreamboat Willy. If the name bothered him, he never showed it.

As a freshman at Eton, William had few special privileges. He was assigned to Manor House where he had a small private room with a small bath over the kitchen. His furniture was a twin bed and a nightstand. A police detective stood guard outside his room whenever he was inside.

Fitting In

William followed the same schedule and wore the same uniform as the other students. The uniform consisted of a formal suit, white button-down shirt, and black vest. He also enjoyed the same after-class activities as the other students. His favorites were soccer, water polo, tennis, rugby, and swimming.

During his school holidays he enjoyed skiing and playing tourist. He especially liked Disney World in Orlando, Florida. Away from school he preferred casual clothing and listening to rock music. His favorite groups at this time were Pulp and the Spice Girls.

Wealth and privilege brought many benefits but could not shield William from family problems.

Prince William plays soccer for his Eton team just days before his eighteenth birthday.

After a separation of several years, Prince Charles and Diana divorced in August 1996.

This would not be the last difficult event William would have to endure. Soon he would face the greatest tragedy of his young life.

CHAPTER THREE

A Public Family Tragedy

The years of friction between Charles and Diana had been difficult on the entire family. The couple tried to spare their sons' feelings. They tried to keep their own conflicts away from the boys. But William and Harry had been well aware of the problems. As in many families, they often heard their parents arguing. Sometimes William heard his mother crying and he would try to comfort her. It was also difficult for William to divide his loyalty between his parents, since he loved them both.

William also worried about his younger brother and spent as much time with Harry as he could. After William went away to school, he worried about his brother having to deal with all of the stress alone.

The formal separation and later the divorce, though sad for the family, at least established a routine

William always had a close relationship with his mother.

for William and his brother. They began alternating their weekends and school holidays between their parents' homes.

With their mother, home life was very relaxed. Sometimes they gathered in her bedroom to watch movies, occasionally snacked on fast food, and wore jeans and T-shirts.

William and Diana had a very easygoing relationship. She teased him about being the object of attention among Britain's young girls. She even nicknamed him DDG for "drop dead gorgeous." This embarrassed William, who asked her not to call him that in public. Diana also valued William's opinion. He suggested that she auction some of her old evening gowns and donate the proceeds to AIDS research. Diana liked

Prince Charles and his son ride a ski lift in Switzerland.

William's idea and did as he suggested. The well-publicized auction was very successful.

Life with their father was more reserved. Charles preferred for his sons to wear blazers and slacks and to have more structured meals at the table. His approach to parenting was more formal than Diana's. But William also enjoyed the time he spent with his father. They enjoyed riding and hunting together. Contrary to some reports, Charles was a loving and devoted father. A great tragedy would soon make this relationship even more important.

The Accident

While on a summer holiday from school in July 1997, William and Harry traveled to the south of France with their mother as the guests of Mohammed al Fayed, a family friend. They played, swam, and relaxed—a carefree time for the boys and their mother. The only problem was the constant presence of the paparazzi, who took hundreds of photographs to sell to newspapers and tabloids around the world.

Shortly after returning to London, William and Harry traveled to Scotland. They planned to spend time with their father before the start of the next school term.

While in Scotland, William and Harry learned of their mother's death in a car accident. The accident occurred on August 30, 1997. The car carrying Diana, her friend Dodi al Fayed, and Diana's bodyguard had crashed into a support column in a Paris tunnel. An investigation found that their driver had been trying to get away from photographers. Although Diana survived the crash, she died in a Paris hospital the next morning.

The tragedy was well expressed by Lord Jeffrey Archer: "The rest of us have lost a superstar and a very important ambassador. But the children have

A sea of flowers lay in the grass at Kensington Palace as a tribute to the late Princess Diana.

lost their mother. Our hearts should go out to them first."[6]

And so began a period of mourning. At first William and Harry remained in seclusion with their father. A few days after the accident, both boys appeared with their father at the palace in London. They viewed the thousands of flowers that had been left there, shook hands, and thanked the people for their show of love and support. William made no public statements about the accident or his mother's death. All public statements were made by his father, his grandmother, and palace and government officials.

Queen Elizabeth made the official statement for the royal family. She expressed the family's sorrow over Diana's death and their thanks for the outpouring of support shown by her countrymen. But the most heartfelt public statement was made by Prime Minister Tony Blair. "She [Diana] touched the lives of so many others in Britain and throughout the world with joy and comfort. . . . She was the people's princess and that is how she will stay, how she will remain in all our hearts and memories forever."[7]

Two Boys Grieve, a Country Mourns

The funeral service took place September 6, 1997. As the world watched, William, fifteen, and Harry, twelve, walked behind their mother's flag-draped, horse-drawn coffin. With them were their father

Prince Charles, Harry, and William are among those following the gun carriage as Diana's funeral procession makes its way to Westminster Abbey.

and their mother's brother, Charles Spencer (also known as Earl Spencer). Together they walked the three-and-a-half-mile route from Kensington Palace to Westminster Abbey, where the service would be held. The procession took two hours. People along the route carried British flags and threw flowers. The crowd was eerily silent. The most noticeable sounds were the clomping of the horses' hooves on the pavement and the tolling of Westminster's bell.

Dignitaries from around the world filled the pews at Westminster Abbey. As part of the service, one of Diana's friends, Elton John, sang "Good-bye England's Rose," a song he composed especially for the service. The song was a heart-wrenching tribute to their mother, and both boys fought tears. Following the service, William and Harry traveled to Althorp, their mother's family home. She was buried on an island in the middle of a private lake on the estate.

Healing

After the burial William and Harry went with their father to Highgrove. On September 19 Prince Charles made a speech. He urged the press and public to allow his sons the opportunity to grieve for their mother privately. "As many of you will know from the experience of family loss in your own lives, it is inevitably very difficult to cope with grief at any time. But perhaps you might realize it is even harder when the whole world is watching at the same time."[8]

Charles and William walk through the gardens of their home. They have grown closer since Diana's death.

Their father kept them busy riding horses, swimming, and hiking. Prince Charles and William developed an even closer relationship during this time. They took long walks in the privacy of the grounds, and Charles made sure both of his sons knew he

31

would be available for them whenever they needed him. After a week, the boys returned to school. In his luggage William carried his mother's diamond-and-sapphire engagement ring.

Diana and Charles had always done their best to encourage their sons to experience the pleasures of a normal, average childhood, although their circumstances were far from average. They wanted their sons to appreciate their privileges and to help others. As a young adult William would have the opportunity to make use of his parents' teachings.

CHAPTER FOUR

The Present and Beyond

When Prince William graduated from Eton at age eighteen he decided to take a year-long break before starting university. During this year he sought new experiences. He wanted to learn about life in settings far from the money and privilege of his own life. He also decided to test his skills in the wilderness and to spend time with members of Britain's military forces.

New Experiences

Prince William finished Eton in 2000, shortly after his eighteenth birthday. This year away from school would give him a break from public attention and the responsibilities of being a prince. It would also allow him time to travel.

His first stop was the jungles of Belize in Central America. There he joined up with British military

William chops logs during his ten-week expedition to Chile.

forces during their training. He took part in survival exercises with the Welsh Guards. While there, William wore military gear, ate British army rations, and slept in a hammock strung between trees.

William also took part in a ten-week expedition in Chile. This expedition was a mix of wilderness travel and learning about village life in rural Chile. Its three phases included adventure, environment, and community.

On one part of the trip, William went sea kayaking along the Patagonian coast. He and his group became stranded on an isolated beach for five days by heavy rains and gale-force winds. William and his group learned the awesome power of nature firsthand. They were grateful they had been trained for wilderness survival and had brought proper provisions to help them endure their unexpected delay.

On another part of the trip, William helped build walkways in a small village that had no roads. He also taught English to the villagers. William had studied Spanish in school. He enjoyed using his Spanish to talk and play games with the children. William also worked on repairing the roof of the village radio station, where he served as guest DJ.

A Taste of Village Life

As a volunteer in the village, William shared quarters with fifteen others. They spread their sleeping bags on the floor of a former nursery school at night. William also pitched in with the chores, including

Six-year-old Alejandro Heredia rides on William's shoulders at the Tortel nursery in southern Chile.

cooking and cleaning. Their cookstove and source of heat was a wood-burning stove, and the whole group had to share one bathroom.

William took the hardships of the village in stride. "The living conditions here aren't exactly what I'm used to, but they are definitely better than I've had in the past six weeks [in Belize]."[9]

Other adventures included a safari in Africa and working as a farm laborer in England. Of all his experiences during his break, William said his favorite time was his brief stint at farm labor. For a month, he worked alongside other farmhands, rising before dawn to milk cows, muck out stalls, and perform other

Prince William spends a quiet moment during his day of domestic duties in Tortel.

menial tasks. For his work, he received the same wages as the other farmhands, less than five dollars an hour.

But soon his year away from studies was over and Prince William stepped back into the public spotlight.

At University

In the fall of 2001 Prince William entered the University of St. Andrews. Founded in 1411, St. Andrews is the oldest university in Scotland. St. Andrews has a

William shakes hands with admirers outside the Sighthill Community Education Center in Glasgow, Scotland.

St. Salvators Hall, William's dormitory at St. Andrew's University in Scotland.

tradition of academic excellence, and students come to St. Andrews from all over the world.

Before beginning at St. Andrews, William was asked what effect having a future king on campus might have on the school and students.

"It will get easier as time goes on. Everyone will get bored of me—which they do,"[10] he quipped.

St. Andrews appealed to William because it allows him to live outside of England. It also has the small-town feeling where his privacy will be respected and protected. Because of the small-town atmosphere, there is little nightlife. This does not bother Prince William who says he really does not like to party a lot. If William and his friends want entertainment, they can drive into Edinburgh, which is only an hour away by car. However, William's highest priority at this time is his education.

William is still in the early days of his university career. He is studying art history, but has not yet declared his major. He may stay with art history, but he also has indicated an interest in geography.

Someday a King

William's life is, to a great extent, already mapped. He will not be an engineer, an airline pilot, or a doctor. He will one day be king of England. In that role he will attend meetings of Parliament, Britain's governing body. His duties as king will also include state visits to other countries, entertaining official visitors to his country, and maintaining close contact with the prime minister. As king he will head the army, navy, and air force, and serve as patron or president of hundreds of organizations. He will not have any direct power over the government, however. Britain's kings and queens no longer govern but they do have great influence.

The eldest son of the Prince of Wales poses in front of an extinct volcano in Edinburgh, Scotland.

No one knows how long it will be before William is crowned king. His father, Prince Charles, is in his fifties and first in line to rule behind William's grandmother, Queen Elizabeth. To date, Elizabeth has not said when she might step down from the throne and allow Charles to assume the title of king.

In the meantime, William will complete his education at St. Andrews, likely perform a period of military service, and assume more responsibilities connected with his place in the royal family. And someday he will be King William V of England.

NOTES

Chapter One: Always in the Spotlight

1. Quoted in Christopher Anderson, *Diana's Boys: William and Harry and the Mother They Loved.* New York: William Morrow, 2001, p. 46.
2. Quoted in Randi Reisfeld, *Prince William: The Boy Who Will Be King.* New York: Pocket Books, 1997, p. 31.

Chapter Two: Educating a Future King

3. Quoted in Reisfeld, *Prince William*, p. 41.
4. Quoted in Reisfeld, *Prince William*, pp. 47–48.
5. Quoted in Reisfeld, *Prince William*, pp. 87–88.

Chapter Three: A Public Family Tragedy

6. Quoted in Anderson, *Diana's Boys*, p. 226.
7. Quoted in Andrew Morton, *Diana: Her True Story.* New York: Simon & Schuster, 1997, p. 277.
8. Quoted in Anderson, *Diana's Boys*, p. 23.

Chapter Four: The Present and Beyond

9. Quoted in *Prince of Wales*. www.princeofwales.gov.uk.
10. Quoted in *Prince of Wales*. www.princeofwales.gov.uk.

FOR FURTHER EXPLORATION

Books

Jane Billinghurst, *Growing Up Royal: Life in the Shadow of the British Throne*. New York: Annick Press, 2001. Describes the lives of the current royal family of England.

M.E. Crane, *Prince William: A Birthday Scrapbook*. New York: Aladdin Paperback, 2000. A chronology well documented by many colorful photographs.

Michael Johnstone, *Prince William: The Story So Far*. New York: D.K., 1999. A realistic, well-illustrated documentary.

Brook Walters, *Prince William: A Journey to the Throne*. New York: Central Park, 1998. Well documented with large, colorful photographs.

Website

Prince of Wales (www.princeofwales.gov.uk). This is an official website of the royal family. It includes information about Prince William.

INDEX

PICTURE CREDITS

About the Author

Sheila Wyborny lives in Houston, Texas, with her husband. She is a retired teacher, and enjoys reading mysteries and traveling with her husband in their airplane. She likes to hear from students who have read her books.

23.70

jB
WILLIAM   Wyborny, Sheila

Prince William
$23.70

1-04

2004

DEMCO